DR DU BOIS AND MISS OVINGTON

Clare Coss

BROADWAY PLAY PUBLISHING INC
224 E 62nd St, NY NY 10065-8201
212 772-8334 fax: 212 772-8358
BroadwayPlayPubl.com

First printing: October 2014
I S B N: 978-0-88145-620-2

Book design: Marie Donovan
Page make-up: Adobe Indesign
Typeface: Palatino
Printed and bound in the U S A

ABOUT THE AUTHOR

Clare Coss's play, DR DU BOIS AND MISS
OVINGTON was written at the request of Woodie
King, Jr, producer/director of the New Federal
Theatre. Her other plays include: GROWING UP
GOTHIC (Theater for the New City and Interart
Theater); LILLIAN WALD: AT HOME ON HENRY
STREET (commissioned and produced by New
Federal, Lincoln Center Theater on Film and Video
Collection); THE BLESSING (American Place);
OUR PLACE IN TIME: TEN SCENES FROM THE
TWENTIETH CENTURY(Women's Project and
New Federal); THE STAR STRANGLED BANNER
(Berkshire Theatre Festival Barn); STRING OF PEARLS
(Provincetown Theater); co-author with Segal and
Sklar, THE DAUGHTERS CYCLE: DAUGHTERS,
SISTER/SISTER, ELECTRA SPEAKS (Interart Theater,
NEA, NYSCA, CAPS, Joint Foundation Support); THE
WELL OF LIVING WATERS, lyricist and co-author
with Mel Spiegel, original score Thiago de Mello
(Cathedral of Saint John the Divine). SHA-SHA, a radio
play, WBAI Pacifica "Beyond the Pale" archives.

Clare Coss is the author of the prize-winning play,
EMMETT, DOWN IN MY HEART that opened at the
Tucson Alliance of Dramatic Artists (TADA!), February
2014. Preceding TADA!, the play had several staged
readings with Kathleen Chalfant, Danny Glover,
Kenny Leon, Linda Powell, Mercedes Ruehl at The

Culture Project; Chicago's Rivendell Theatre; John Drew Theater, Guild Hall, East Hampton; Judson Church in association with Culture Project. Translated into French, DANS LES RIVIERES DU DELTA, was presented at Moving Parts Theatre in Paris. Coss is collaborating on her libretto, EMMETT TILL, THE OPERA, with composer Mary Watkins.

Coss presents dramatic readings of her one-woman plays LILLIAN WALD: AT HOME ON HENRY STREET, and DANGEROUS TERRITORY (Mary White Ovington). Publications: *Lillian D Wald: Progressive Activist* (Feminist Press) and *The Arc of Love, An Anthology of Lesbian Love Poems* (Scribner), a Lambda Literary Award finalist. She is a member of the League of Professional Theatre Women, Dramatists Guild, PEN, Columbia University Seminar on Women and Society. Coss served on Thanks Be To Grandmother Winifred Foundation Board, and for ten years was Poetry Editor for *Affilia*. www.ClareCoss.com

DR DU BOIS AND MISS OVINGTON was first
presented as a staged reading in The National Black
Touring Circuit's Black History Month Play Series 2013
(Woodie King, Jr, Producer) in association with Castillo
Theatre. The cast and creative contributor were:

MISS OVINGTON.......................................Kathleen Chalfant
DR DU BOIS.. Peter Jay Fernandez

Director... Gabrielle Kurlander

DR DU BOIS AND MISS OVINGTON was produced
by New Federal Theatre (Woodie King Jr, Producer)
in association with Castillo Theatre (Dan Friedman,
Artistic Director; Diane Stiles, Managing Director) in
New York. The play opened on 17 January 2014. The
cast and creative contributors were:

MISS OVINGTON.......................................Kathleen Chalfant
DR DU BOIS... Timothy Simonson

Director... Gabrielle Kurlander
Choreographer... Lonne Moretton
Production stage manager .... Bayo
Set design .... Chris Cumberbatch
Light design .... Antoinette Tynes
Costume design .... Ali Turns
Sound design... Bill Toles
Technical director................................... Anthony Davidson

CHARACTERS

DR DU BOIS (WILLIAM EDWARD BURGHARDT [W E B])
February 23, 1868—August 27, 1963
Du Bois pronounced "Due BOYS"
Addressed as "Dr" after earning his PhD at Harvard.
Nickname: Will
Forty-seven, African-American, married, race rights
visionary and activist, co-founder N A A C P, historian,
sociologist, author, editor, Pan-Africanist
Imperious, aggressive, passionate, spontaneous, likes to tease

MISS OVINGTON (MARY WHITE OVINGTON)
April 11, 1865—July 15, 1951
Nickname: May
Fifty, white, single, anti-racist visionary and activist, co-
founder N A A C P, suffragist, socialist, pacifist, settlement
house founder, author, journalist
Earnest, strong-willed, passionate, nurturing, likes to tease

SETTING

Time: A late June Sunday morning 1915

Place: National Association for the Advancement of Colored People (N A A C P) Office, 70 Fifth Avenue, New York City. (A tall white building owned by Ginn & Co, Publishers.) The office is light and airy with a wall of windows looking over the avenue. It has a busy look, with fliers, pamphlets, The Crisis Magazine, *books stacked here and there.*

Westminster Clock Chimes: They are heard from a nearby church tower. They chime on the hour and each quarter hour. As the scene opens at 10 A M in the N A A C P office, the full melody plays, followed by ten strikes. The melody progresses each quarter hour, back to full, followed by eleven strikes, and on to the quarter hour and half hour melodies.

INTRODUCTORY NOTES

MARY WHITE OVINGTON (1865-1951), granddaughter of Connecticut abolitionists , raised in an affluent Brooklyn Unitarian family, was a writer, feminist, socialist, pacifist, suffragist. She attended the Harvard Annex for two years. A progressive social worker and community organizer, Ovington invited Booker T Washington to speak to New York City's Social Reform Club about conditions for black communities in the North. His words: "The Negro is completely outside the work and vision of the reformers" inspired her to become the first white woman to dedicate her life to anti-racist work in the twentieth century. My one-woman play on Mary White Ovington, DANGEROUS TERRITORY, reveals her compelling story, boldly to demand equality and justice for all Americans. Segregation, economic and educational inequality, lynchings, continual sparks of outrage, notably the Springfield, Illinois, Race Riot of 1908, led her to imagine and help build the National Association for the Advancement of Colored People (N A A C P) in 1909. Considered a pioneering experiment, it was the first time black and white activists worked together for justice and equality. In 1903 Ovington, deeply moved by Du Bois's prophetic collection of essays on black consciousness and activism, *The Souls Of Black Folk*, wrote to him. Their correspondence and friendship grew into a working

alliance that defined the NAACP and enabled it to
survive.

WILLIAM EDWARD BURGHARDT DU BOIS
(1868–1963), leading twentieth century intellectual and
activist, was born in Great Barrington, Massachusetts,
the great-grandson of an enslaved African, Tom
Burghardt, who gained his freedom as a soldier in
the American Revolution. Du Bois, a graduate of Fisk
University and the first African-American to earn
a PhD from Harvard University, was a writer, Pan-
Africanist, sociologist, historian, educator, editor.
His influential works concerned the oppression and
exploitation of African-Americans and all people of
color, the importance of African history and culture,
and the struggle for total equality. Du Bois's many
writings are enlivened by satire, humor, and a burning
outrage at injustice. Co-founder of The Niagara
Movement in 1905, the first organized response since
Reconstruction actively to demand equal justice, the
organization renounced Booker T Washington's policy
of accommodation. Their manifesto demanded the
vote, an end to discrimination, and the same liberties
afforded white citizens. Underfunded and denied
press coverage, members of Niagara joined with
white progressives to create the N A A C P in 1909. A
member of the integrated board, Du Bois became the
first African-American to serve in the Administration
of the N A A C P. As editor of the organization's
magazine, *The Crisis*, he devoted each monthly issue
with his "militant" mission: civil rights for black
Americans and people of color in the U.S. and around
the world.

For Audre Lorde

"It is not our differences that divide us. It is our inability to recognize, accept, and celebrate those differences."

Audre Lorde, *Our Dead Behind Us: Poems*

(Opening scene)

(The D S lights come up to reveal DR DU BOIS, *D S R and* MISS OVINGTON, *D S L, at separate speaking engagements. He stands next to his Lantern Slide Projector.* MISS OVINGTON *sits on a cushioned pew in the Mount Zion A M E Church in Woolwich Township, New Jersey. A pulpit is to one side. The stage set is dark and unseen behind them. Their last lines and first lines follow quickly as the focus shifts between them.)*

DR DU BOIS: It is a great pleasure to speak at Oberlin College, where students are admitted on merit, not on the color of their skin. I am enthralled with viewing the photograph through my new Lantern Slide Projector. You will be, too. These images portray deep and bitter wrongs we black folk face every day.

(As DR DU BOIS *speaks, he opens a small wooden box that contains ten glass plates, each with a different image. He slides a plate into the machine, identifies the image as it is projected on the front drop screen behind him.)*

DR DU BOIS: A Public Library. We are denied entry.

(Next plate)

DR DU BOIS: Public swimming pool in the Bronx. Black children outside the fence look in. Denied entry.

(Next plate)

DR DU BOIS: Playground in a park. Outside the fence black children watch white children swing, see-saw, slide, climb on the jungle gym. Denied entry.

(Next plate)

DR DU BOIS: Elevator in the Wall Street district. It could as well be a Park Avenue residence.

MISS OVINGTON: *(Music begins to overlap his last image as the focus shifts to* MISS OVINGTON *enjoying the church choir.)*
We're on our way
and we won't turn back
We're on our way
and we won't turn back
We're on our way
and we won't turn back
We're on our way
o YES, we're on our way.
(She rises and walks to the pulpit.) Good morning, New Jersey neighbors. The tide was with me on the ferry ride across the Hudson.

CHORAL RESPONSE: Good morning.

MISS OVINGTON: It is an honor to speak in your church, once a stop on the Underground Railroad. Your minister posed a frequently asked question: Who are you, Miss Ovington? What led you to devote your life to anti-racist work?

DR DU BOIS: *(The focus shifts back to him. Next plate)* A N Y C Labor Union Meeting. Skilled black men and women, denied membership.
Woodrow Wilson, our first southern president since the Civil War, has re-segregated federal office buildings. Here—

(Next plate)

DR DU BOIS: The U S Post Office. Colored workers must climb stairs to the 8th floor to use one designated toilet.

MISS OVINGTON: *(The focus shifts back to her.)* When Booker Washington spoke to the Social Reform Club in 1903, he leaned forward to confide, "Colored New Yorkers are the most neglected in your city, completely outside your vision." I stared at him stunned.

DR DU BOIS: *(The lights shift the focus back to him Next plate)* The U S Treasury Building—Negro workers are kept behind screens and closed doors as if they are lepers. Secretary of the Treasury McAdoo, "Ku Ku McAdoo", believes segregation eases racial tension and protects colored employees.

MISS OVINGTON: *(The focus shifts back to her.)* Who are my colleagues of another race? Why have I never met them? Why aren't they here at the Social Reform Club? I had an epiphany! His words ignited in me the need for dramatic change!

DR DU BOIS: *(The focus shifts back to him. Next plate)* Washington's lovely Rock Creek Park—Whites Only—

(Next plate)

DR DU BOIS: Ice Cream Parlor in our nation's capitol— Whites Only—

(Last plate)

DR DU BOIS: A cemetery—anywhere U S A. Keep the black man and the white man far apart—even in death.

(DR DU BOIS and MISS OVINGTON each pose face front for "a photographer." A big white flash and 'poof' goes off. They turn and exit S R and S L respectively. His table and her pulpit are cleared. An instrumental reprise of "We're On Our Way" plays through the transition.)

(*The N A A C P headquarters office set is revealed, bathed in a bright sunny morning light pouring in from the tall bank of windows S L.*)

(*On the back wall is a large map of the United States. At the top are the words : LET US BEAR WITNESS. LYNCHINGS 1915. Stick pins mark the site of lynchings across the country. The South is thick with pins. There is a Gramaphone [Victor's Talking Machine] with a large speaker and a candlestick telephone on a small table D S L.*)

(*Three quarters of the stage from L to beyond C R is the main office. S R is the front of DR DU BOIS's office. S R MISS OVINGTON's desk in the main office faces his desk, separated by the "wall" of his office. Next to his desk a Dictophone machine with a long speaking tube sits on a small secretary's desk, a head set hanging on the back of her chair. The door to his office is to the right of her desk. The front entrance door is D R.*)

(*MISS OVINGTON, tall, slender, attractive, unlocks the door, enters, unpins her straw hat and hangs it up on a tall wooden hat stand next to the door. She is wearing an attractive pale green ankle length summer dress. She relocks the door as Westminster bell chimes ring out the hour melody from a nearby church, followed by ten strikes to mark the hour.*)

(*MISS OVINGTON picks up a packet of mail from the drop box hanging low on the front door, places it on her desk and quickly sorts it into two piles while standing. With an urgency, she pulls the cover off of her Remington typewriter, sits down and rolls in a blank page of paper to begin typing.*)

MISS OVINGTON: (*Types and speaks in an angry voice*)
Dear Chairman Spingarn:
Your antagonism at yesterday's board meeting astonished me.
YOU seek to wreck our cause—not Dr Du Bois.
(*Stops typing*) Ahh! Friction! Friction! Friction! (*She tears*

*the paper out of the typewriter, crumples and throws it in
the waste basket. Rolls in a fresh sheet of paper, reflects for a
moment.)*

(Abruptly MISS OVINGTON *stands up, checks a page of the
folded Sunday* New York Times. *She picks up a pushpin
from a bowl on her desk, then marches over to the wall map,
reaches up to press the pin into a heavily pinned spot in
Alabama.)*

*(*DR DU BOIS, *handsome with a formal air, unlocks the door,
enters quietly, sets down a small suitcase. He is surprised
to see her hat on the stand. Listens. All is quiet, except for
the church bells. He is wearing a light blue seersucker suit,
white shirt, vest, spats on his polished leather shoes. He
carries a smart walking stick. He hangs up his panama hat
next to her hat. As he rounds the corner He is startled to see
*MISS OVINGTON *at the map. He watches her press in the pin
and "a-hems" to alert her to his presence.)*

MISS OVINGTON: *(Turns her head quickly, startled)* Oh! Dr
Du Bois!

DR DU BOIS: *(Puzzled to see her there)* Miss Ovington!
Why are you in the office on a Sunday morning?

MISS OVINGTON: To save the N A A C P! Why are you
here?

DR DU BOIS: To revise my resignation letter!

MISS OVINGTON: You cannot resign!

DR DU BOIS: I most certainly can and shall!

*(*MISS OVINGTON *turns back to the map.* DR DU BOIS
*watches her press a pin into Alabama. They speak in clipped
tones.)*

DR DU BOIS: Yet another lynching.

MISS OVINGTON: Alabama.

DR DU BOIS: The Negro hater flourishes in the land.
Blackness is the crime of crimes.

MISS OVINGTON: White indifference is the crime of crimes. *(She turns to face him)* Please, Dr Du Bois, look at me.

DR DU BOIS: *(They exchange a brief steady gaze.)* Do not expect to engage me in mollifying conversation. *(Gruffly, he turns and enters his office.)* I will be speaking into the Dictaphone.

MISS OVINGTON: Oh, you will be shaving your wax cylinder.

DR DU BOIS: You find that amusing, Miss Ovington?

MISS OVINGTON: Why not speak directly to me. *(Picks up* The Crisis, *waves it) The Crisis* just out. Lovely art work and features. Excellent *Birth of a Nation* editorial—

DR DU BOIS: *(He nods with thanks, steps to his door.)* With your permission—I am closing the door—

MISS OVINGTON: I will be pounding on the Remington— *(Pointedly)* —for the future life of our organization, our partnership.

DR DU BOIS: *(Taps indicating his inside breast pocket)* Miss Ovington, my resignation letter resides right here, next to my heart. That I can whip it out at any moment sustains me.

MISS OVINGTON: What are we up to—four? Is it four now? Is this your fourth resignation letter?

DR DU BOIS: Yes, my fourth since you are counting. And last. The board's new demands attempt to force me into a position of servitude.

MISS OVINGTON: Yesterday's board meeting—all that unbridled animosity—I could not sleep last night.

DR DU BOIS: I came in to dictate revisions to my resignation letter for Miss Randolph to type out.

MISS OVINGTON: Do you not want to talk over the contentious issues that plague—

DR DU BOIS: *(Interrupting)* They are insoluble. For five years of our existence I have put up with the board's efforts to control me.

MISS OVINGTON: Fate has thrown us together now. Let us take advantage of this propitious moment. What are your specific demands?

DR DU BOIS: You will see when Miss Randolph posts them to the board in the morning.

MISS OVINGTON: If you resign, or they drive you out, what does that say. See. Black and white cannot work together. Not even in the leadership of the N A A C P.

(DR DU BOIS turns to enter his office.)

MISS OVINGTON: Here, you and I unite against the greatest odds, because we value the worth of every single human being. We must not fail.

DR DU BOIS: *(He turns back to her.)* We must not fail, for our task is to transform three hundred years of alienation between black and white in our country— and stir a great awakening in the American Negro—an inner revolution. The magic, the absolutism of the word "white" is breaking. Excuse me, Miss Ovington. *(He closes his door, picks up the wax cylinder and begins to shave it.)*

(MISS OVINGTON stands looking at his closed door, frustrated and upset. She hears the sound of a fife and drum playing "Yankee Doodle." Chants are heard over the music: "Be prepared!" "Men to Arms!". She goes to the window and looks down, not liking what she sees. She turns back into the office and picks up a long wooden flagpole leaning next to the map, and drags it to the window.)

(DR DU BOIS stops shaving the cylinder and listens. As MISS OVINGTON lifts the pole, the banner unfurls to reveal

*in large letters: "A Man Was Lynched Yesterday." She
drags the step ladder over to the window. He stops again and
listens, then opens his door.)*

MISS OVINGTON: Look! Militarists! Drumming for us to
enter Europe's unnecessary war.

DR DU BOIS: *(Joining her at the window)* Europe's
scramble to dominate the darker peoples.

MISS OVINGTON: And make the rich richer on
armaments. *(Shouts out of the window)* End the War!
Keep the U S neutral!

("Men to Arms! Men to Arms!" is called out on the street.)

DR DU BOIS: *(Stands at the window, calls out)* Men to
thievery, assassination, rape, torture, murder—the
white man's deviltry on the African continent! *(To
her)* Even so we must be certain our Negro boys break
through the color line and are allowed to join up and
prove themselves.

MISS OVINGTON: So they too can be slaughtered on
foreign soil. *(Shouts out of the window)* End the war!
Keep the U S neutral!

DR DU BOIS: Our neutrality won't last. Miss Ovington,
our nation will jump on the band wagon of greed and
empire.

MISS OVINGTON: The neutral nations are trying to end
the war. Our peace movement's big model dinosaur
shows what happens when we become too heavily
armed for our own good. Extinction.

DR DU BOIS: Asia, Africa, India will be colonized to the
hilt. If the slave cannot be taken from Africa, slavery
can now be taken to Africa.

MISS OVINGTON: *(Admiringly)* That is brilliant. The
concept. *(She picks up the flagpole and banner.)* Yet you

would have our young colored men march into the jaws of Molloch.

(The Fife and Drum band begins to fade away.)

(MISS OVINGTON *starts up the stepladder holding the flagpole.)*

DR DU BOIS: Do you have to hang the flag out now?

MISS OVINGTON: Our banner: A Man Was Lynched Yesterday. Streams of Sunday churchgoers stroll on the avenue below. A reminder to love thy neighbor.

DR DU BOIS: I will do it.

MISS OVINGTON: No, I've done it before. Dropping the pole into the stand is tricky.

DR DU BOIS: *(He gingerly puts his arms around her waist to hold her.)* Do not fall out the window.

MISS OVINGTON: *(She slides the pole in the stand on the outside window frame. The flag hangs straight out. She loses her balance and he catches her, his arms around her waist. A sudden spark ignites between them.)* Hello.

DR DU BOIS: Hello.

(DR DU BOIS lets go, steps back, offers his hand as MISS OVINGTON steps down the ladder.)

MISS OVINGTON: Thank you for holding on to me.

DR DU BOIS: Well I do not want you to go flying on a Sunday morning.

MISS OVINGTON: Your Miss Fauset sets out the flag. She is young and agile.

DR DU BOIS: She is not MY Miss Fauset. She is OUR Literary Editor.

MISS OVINGTON: *(Leans out of the window, looks down)* Look—how easily our banner catches the eye.

(MISS OVINGTON *waves to a stranger on the street.* DR DU BOIS *leans out of the window with her.*)

MISS OVINGTON: A refreshing breeze—

DR DU BOIS: *(Crisply)* Some of the fortunate few still in town.

(DR DU BOIS *and* MISS OVINGTON *turn back into the room. She leans against the window sill.*)

MISS OVINGTON: I do not know why you are gruff and imperious with me. I supported you down the line yesterday. I even lost my temper for the first time defending you.

DR DU BOIS: Bravo.

MISS OVINGTON: You never lose your temper.

DR DU BOIS: I never will.

MISS OVINGTON: Well, bravo. *(Slight pause)* I cannot believe you drove me to attack our colleagues. "I can get along with Dr Du Bois! I do not know what the matter is with the rest of you!"

DR DU BOIS: You spoke truth.

MISS OVINGTON: When I apologized to Chairman Spingarn after the meeting—I should not tell you this.

DR DU BOIS: Should not? Then you must.

MISS OVINGTON: Fanning the flames—

DR DU BOIS: What did he say?

MISS OVINGTON: He accused me—of being—an "idolator."

(DR DU BOIS *laughs heartily.*)

MISS OVINGTON: It is not funny.

DR DU BOIS: A Unitarian—accused of being an "idolator?"

(DR DU BOIS *laughs.* MISS OVINGTON *laughs reluctantly.*)

DR DU BOIS: What prompted that?

MISS OVINGTON: Oh—a praise song.

DR DU BOIS: Tell me.

MISS OVINGTON: You do not need to know everything.

DR DU BOIS: Of course I do.

MISS OVINGTON: I said, "Dr Du Bois is a genius. We are all journeymen next to him."

DR DU BOIS: Mmm—hmm.

MISS OVINGTON: But now the genius prefers to dictate to a machine rather than search for a solution with a warm blooded living human being.

DR DU BOIS: All right. Very well. My demands. One. I refuse Chairman Spingarn's proposal to monitor my time. I have to write articles, books, travel the lecture circuit to generate income since my salary here is a pittance.

MISS OVINGTON: You have my unequivocal support on this point. I made that clear yesterday.

DR DU BOIS: Two. I must have complete autonomy as Editor of *The Crisis*.

MISS OVINGTON: Not new.

DR DU BOIS: No not new. Not by any means new.

MISS OVINGTON: I know that is what you want.

DR DU BOIS: Not what I want, Miss Ovington, what I need. It is not negotiable. The board is not my overseer on what I choose to publish.

MISS OVINGTON: There are board members, black and white, who claim you to be the source of friction, disorder, and lack of unity in our organization.

DR DU BOIS: They want to stifle all initiative on my part but use my name as editor.

MISS OVINGTON: They want to eliminate you.

DR DU BOIS: So they can popularize *The Crisis* to say nothing anyone can disagree with. Either my position is one of real dignity and decision making, or any clerk can do the job. This is my chance to do a big piece of work—to foster the freeing of ten million Negro souls—who open the mailbox and find a lifeline to dignity and self-respect. And insight. And possibility. *(Slight pause)* Miss Ovington, the board accuses me of being "childish and insubordinate," and instructs me to report to an Advisory Committee of three who will pass judgment on my editorials and expenses. Demeaning! Outrageous! I report only to the full board, not a special Committee of Three. You know what the real problem is.

MISS OVINGTON: What?

DR DU BOIS: They refuse to share power with a Negro!

MISS OVINGTON: They ARE sharing power with you. They are just not used to it.

DR DU BOIS: Miss Ovington, they are not sharing power with me. They fight me every step of the way. Surely you see that. You, Miss Ovington, of all people, the only white person I know who has crossed the color line. You, who lived in a model tenement on a block of five thousand Negro citizens. You know the color line when you see it. That is the rift in this organization.

MISS OVINGTON: We must not let the color line tear us apart. We are pioneers in a great experiment. I have worked steadily to prevent personal attacks. Yesterday—regrettably—it all broke down.

DR DU BOIS: You know the big risk I took leaving Atlanta University for this activist mission. To convince my black and whitened race of their right to demand freedom and justice. To inspire them to do it! I have faith in my people. I want *The Crisis* to change lives. To liberate human beings out of slavery. To liberate heart, mind, soul.

MISS OVINGTON: You are our visionary.

DR DU BOIS: Not to our colleagues who would prefer an all white organization rather than make room for a Negro who is not subservient.

MISS OVINGTON: We are a team here. Why do you act unilaterally. You rented a larger office for *The Crisis* without consulting anyone. Why did you not propose a new office at the board meeting?

DR DU BOIS: Indeed! To suffer endless debate and rejection? Why?

MISS OVINGTON: I can get along with you perfectly well, except, except—

DR DU BOIS: Except—except—

MISS OVINGTON: Why do you refuse to reign in your temperament.

DR DU BOIS: I do not doubt in the least that my temperament is difficult to endure. In my peculiar education and experiences it would be miraculous if I came through normal and unwarped.

MISS OVINGTON: Why do you insist on making people angry or miserable?

DR DU BOIS: Let them be angry or miserable. *The Crisis* pays for itself! Thirty thousand in circulation and climbing! Is this disorganization, hindrance, lack of cooperation of which I am accused? The Association cannot exist without my journal.

MISS OVINGTON: The Association cannot exist without you.

(MISS OVINGTON *walks over to the window,* DR DU BOIS *follows her.*)

MISS OVINGTON: If we cannot solve this, where will you go?

DR DU BOIS: Atlanta has closed its doors. Teaching at Wilberforce was a stroke of luck.

MISS OVINGTON: What will you do?

DR DU BOIS: I sought with bare hands to lift the earth and create my path. *The Crisis*, is like an expression of myself and is intended for my people, a journal to action such as black folk have not dared dream. It is my base. It sustains me. *(Slight pause)* I put the same question to you. What will you do?

MISS OVINGTON: If we fail, the power and energy swirling inside will burn me to pieces. I need to be totally absorbed in work for justice and dignity. *(Slight pause, sincerely)* I want you to be able to work naturally and happily here.

DR DU BOIS: The vexatious limitations of our colleagues make that impossible.

(MISS OVINGTON *turns away, deflated.* DR DU BOIS *quickly strides into his office. He pauses, hesitates, picks up a phonograph record , a peace offering, and returns to her.*)

DR DU BOIS: Miss Ovington, a miracle. You must hear this. *(He goes to the phonograph, cranks it up, carefully sets the record in place. Lifts the phonograph arm.)* A new needle?

MISS OVINGTON: Yes—changed this week.

DR DU BOIS: *(He sets the arm back down.)* In Great Barrington there was only the occasional Negro in a sea of white strangers. Once on a boyhood trip to Rocky Point, Rhode Island, I came upon hundreds of my people gathered together for a holiday. I was dazzled with wonder at their sportive mood, exquisite range of skin color, utter equality of spirit. Later I heard for the first time a chorus of Southern Negroes sing spirituals. Moved to tears, I recognized something inherently and deeply my own. *(He lifts the arm and places the needle carefully on the record. Announces:)* The Fisk Jubilee Singers.

(DR DU BOIS and MISS OVINGTON lean on the windowsill, close to each other, and listen rapturously.)

PHONOGRAPH:
I've been buked and I've been scorned, yes
I've been buked and I've been scorned, children
I've been buked and I've been scorned,
I've been talked about, show's you're born

MISS OVINGTON: *(When she speaks, he turns down the volume.)* Imagine. An entire chorus, right here in our office. Thank you.

DR DU BOIS: *(He looks at her directly)* Does our survival hinge on my temperament.

MISS OVINGTON: Or on my ingenuity?

(MISS OVINGTON looks at DR DU BOIS and smiles, then he smiles. There is a charged moment between them.)

DR DU BOIS: We are very much alike.

MISS OVINGTON: Oh no we are not.

(DR DU BOIS and MISS OVINGTON lean with their backs against the windowsill next to each other.)

MISS OVINGTON: Where are you off to this afternoon.

DR DU BOIS: A speaking engagement in the Berkshires—the land of my birth laced with tender memories of youth.

MISS OVINGTON: You know I love the mountains, too. I spent my childhood summers in New Hampshire.

DR DU BOIS: Where you had your first epiphany, baptized in Nature's peace?

MISS OVINGTON: *(Laughs lightly)* Yes.

(DR DU BOIS turns up the volume and he and MISS OVINGTON listen to the last line of the chorus)

PHONOGRAPH:
I BEEN TALKED ABOUT SHOW'S YOU're born.

(The song over, HE takes the record off, and slides it back in the jacket.)

DR DU BOIS: Why come in this morning and not work in your home office? Is something wrong in Brooklyn, your dear mother?

MISS OVINGTON: It is impossible to work there with our talkative young houseguest from Liberia, Dihdwo Twe *(Pronounced: DEED woe tway)*. He is visiting mother and me for a couple of weeks.

DR DU BOIS: Dihdwo Twe, a mellifluous sound. Do you know the meaning?

MISS OVINGTON: His grandmother named him at birth to reunite the family. Dihdwo Twe, she said —Peace is planted between us.

DR DU BOIS: Lovely. The grace and splendor of our motherlands— *(Sings gently)*
Do bana coba, gene me, gene me!
Do bana coba, gene me, gene me!
Ben d'nuli, ben d'le.

MISS OVINGTON: *(Entranced)* An echo—from your ancient homeland—

DR DU BOIS: My great great grandmother clasped her knees, rocked and crooned her Wolof song.

MISS OVINGTON: Can we return to your demands after that?

DR DU BOIS: I will not report to a Committee of Three. *(He suddenly has a new idea.)* Unless you are on it.

MISS OVINGTON: Out of the question! What a terrible idea! Absolutely impossible!

DR DU BOIS: I know that puts you in an untenable position.

MISS OVINGTON: Dr Du Bois, wouldn't you like to take off your jacket in this heat?

DR DU BOIS: No, I am all right.

MISS OVINGTON: Why not be comfortable?

DR DU BOIS: I am used to being uncomfortable.

MISS OVINGTON: If you were here alone, if I weren't here, you would not stand on ceremony.

DR DU BOIS: You are here.

MISS OVINGTON: Please.

(DR DU BOIS slips off his jacket.)

MISS OVINGTON: I like summer seersucker—such a carefree fabric.

(DR DU BOIS hangs it on the back of the desk chair.)

MISS OVINGTON: You do not have to take off your spats.

(DR DU BOIS and MISS OVINGTON laugh.)

DR DU BOIS: Thank you.

MISS OVINGTON: May I speak frankly, Dr Du Bois?

DR DU BOIS: You are going to heat it up even more.

MISS OVINGTON: There is something the matter with *The Crisis* from the viewpoint of white readers.

(DR DU BOIS stares at MISS OVINGTON in silence.)

MISS OVINGTON: As the N A A C P magazine, it serves two races. But its psychology is that of the colored race. *(Slight pause)* You offend white people by calling them hogs and reactionary heathens in your editorials. Listen to this sentence—

DR DU BOIS: Oh, come come, Miss Ovington.

MISS OVINGTON: It is open to the page because I was going to write to you. *(Reads from* The Crisis*)* "It takes extraordinary training, gift and opportunity to make the average white man anything but an overbearing hog, but the most ordinary Negro is an instinctive gentleman." What does that say to our readers? Why insult our white constituency? *(Slight pause)* Dr Du Bois, no one can be more persuasive than you before a white audience, or can write more persuasively for white people. But with *The Crisis* that white audience is sometimes forgotten and its feelings are badly hurt.

DR DU BOIS: Was I not even handed when I criticized the black church and their ministerial ranks choked with pretentious ill-trained men? They inveigh against dancing, the theatre, blame educated people for objecting to their empty sermons.

MISS OVINGTON: That editorial confounded our entire board. Just when we were starting out, intending to build up our ranks through the churches, you attack them and accuse many of dishonesty.

Then you targeted the black colleges for nepotism and being out of step with advances in higher education. Who could believe, you went on to attack the Negro press for anti-intellectualism and bad grammar.

Our board was apoplectic and voted a resolution of appreciation for the Negro press.

DR DU BOIS: I printed the board's placatory resolution, did I not?

MISS OVINGTON: Yes. You ultimately did.

DR DU BOIS: Agitation is necessary to tell the ills of the suffering. If you wish to avoid criticism: Do nothing. Say nothing. Be nothing.

MISS OVINGTON: Your editorial denouncing Theodore Roosevelt's *Brazil and the Negro*—

DR DU BOIS: *(Interrupting)* Oh, no!!! No no no!!! May God deliver us from our white friends who are likely to lynch our souls. Don't antagonize, don't be bitter; say the conciliatory thing; make friends and do not repel them; insist on and emphasize the cheerful and good and dwell as little as possible on wrong and evil.

MISS OVINGTON: I take your point. *(Slight pause)* There is one other thing. *The Crisis* is our official publication. We need more vigorous reporting on branch members out there plowing the ground.

DR DU BOIS: Did you read my feature on Kathryn Magnolia Johnson? She and other branch leaders are struggling to enlighten and arouse local communities to form branches.

MISS OVINGTON: I have reports that she puts off liberal sympathetic whites and the cultured black community. They feel she does not quite represent our Association.

DR DU BOIS: I object to their elitist complaint that Miss Johnson lacks refinement and polish. We enlist members across class lines, do we not, my dear socialist ally? Miss Johnson is a good organizer. She travels without eating or sleeping to avoid the worst humiliations of Jim Crow.

MISS OVINGTON: Miss Johnson is very brave.

DR DU BOIS: Quite. The branches ARE represented in the N A A C P segment.

MISS OVINGTON: How about moving the N A A C P section to the front of the magazine rather than the back pages.

DR DU BOIS: *The Crisis* will be one of the great journals of the world. It is not a newsletter.

MISS OVINGTON: I am not suggesting a newsletter.

DR DU BOIS: *(Serious threat)* Be forewarned, Miss Ovington. This time I will leave the Association if my full conditions are not met. Nothing you say will convince me to stay.

MISS OVINGTON: What is the wisest way for us to proceed?

DR DU BOIS: The wisest way is for us to be honest with each other. You know you agree with me. You know you do. You are more radical than I am in some ways. You introduced me to socialism.

MISS OVINGTON: My mother said you and I are a perfect team.

DR DU BOIS: Your mother is from the moon.

MISS OVINGTON: She will like that, coming from you.

DR DU BOIS: She will?

MISS OVINGTON: You and I have always been able to progress in spite of our inequities.

DR DU BOIS: Which inequities.

MISS OVINGTON: You have the advantage of being male. You have the vote.

DR DU BOIS: You have the advantage of being white— an overall dominance.

MISS OVINGTON: You—never mind.

DR DU BOIS: I what?

MISS OVINGTON: Never mind. It is none of my business.

DR DU BOIS: If it is about me, it is my business. You do that repeatedly. You hint—

MISS OVINGTON: *(Interrupts)* No, I do not.

DR DU BOIS: Yes, you do.

MISS OVINGTON: Well, I do not mean to.

DR DU BOIS: You were saying—

MISS OVINGTON: Now I'm embarrassed. All right—you as a male, have the freedom to fly and flutter from flower to flower.

DR DU BOIS: Oh?

MISS OVINGTON: Well, you do.

DR DU BOIS: That is true. But you, too, as an unmarried woman, have the freedom to fly and flutter.

MISS OVINGTON: Women, especially young women, can get caught. *(Slight pause, then quickly)* There is a violent opposition to our birth control movement.

DR DU BOIS: *(Bows)* I grant you that.

MISS OVINGTON: Women have to fight to be taken seriously. I as a woman could not enter the Harvard Library without written permission from my professor.

DR DU BOIS: I did not know that.

MISS OVINGTON: I had to leave the Harvard Annex after two years because of the economic depression. There were no scholarships for women.

DR DU BOIS: My education depended on scholarships, from my little Berkshire high school on. *(Slight pause)* Well, now you enjoy an inherited legacy—small but sufficient. You draw no salary for your work here. I live hand to mouth. Even with my distinguished Harvard PhD.

MISS OVINGTON: You are brilliant and you are expected to write. Women get no encouragement.

DR DU BOIS: Your Half a Man study is duly recognized. Your recent series on Hayti—illuminating!

Your steadily published short pieces—

MISS OVINGTON: My short pieces. If I were to write authentically and poignantly of my life, as you have done and do so eloquently, who would read it? You, as a man, do not have to rationalize the telling of your life. Women have to make the case for telling our lives.

DR DU BOIS: You bring to mind my mother who existed not for herself but for me. Her sacrifice propelled me forward to do my best. Mother and I were good chums. She died when I was in my teens, her brown velvet skin, sorrowful black-brown eyes, waves of midnight hair—are warm and vivid.

MISS OVINGTON: Your mother would be well pleased with you and your writings on behalf of colored women. *(Slight pause)* Dr Du Bois, whom do you trust? Is Miss Fauset your confidante for everyday hurts and triumphs and—decisions.

DR DU BOIS: Perhaps. To some extent. I imagine on a daily basis you talk with your mother, Louise.

MISS OVINGTON: I am her maiden lady daughter. No matter I lecture across the country, write books, articles, found settlement houses—but without a male authority in my personal life, I am not complete. That's why she likes our partnership. She sees you as—the man in my life.

DR DU BOIS: A man. Not a race man. Is she losing—?

MISS OVINGTON: No. She is compos mentis. The good times she has had with my visitors from around the country and the world have worn away HER color line.

DR DU BOIS: My compliments to your mother. Only once in a large public venue did I feel like a man, not a race man—a man.

MISS OVINGTON: The London Races Congress, where you waltzed with the most beautiful woman in the world, Madameoiselle Legitime, the daughter of

Hayti's president. She spoke a divine French. Do you
not think French is the language of heaven? Ne pensez-
vous pas que le francais est une langue celeste?

DR DU BOIS: Absolument! My Negro blood runs with
a strain of French and Haitian on my father, Alfred Du
Bois' side, a bit of Dutch on my mother, Mary Silvana's
side, but thank God! no "Anglo-Saxon".

MISS OVINGTON: Please please, no attacks on the weary
Anglo-Saxon. It is my own rebellious bloodline—my
abolitionist Connecticut grandparents—

DR DU BOIS: I claim Hayti, home of Toussaint
L'Overture's overthrow of Napoleon and France. Vivre
la Hayti! The third great revolution for humanity.

MISS OVINGTON: I claim a stream of John Brown's
Anglo-Saxon spirit! "The cost of freedom is less than
the price of oppression!" Long Live John Brown!
(Slight pause) At the Races Congress, when we visited
Warwick Castle, I watched Madameoiselle Legitime
lift a peacock feather from the ground and wave it
gracefully as she walked with you arm in arm across
the wide greensward.

DR DU BOIS: You spent an hour under the ancient
Cedars of Lebanon, up on the knoll, with the Sioux
Indian physician—

MISS OVINGTON: You took notice of my whereabouts?

DR DU BOIS: Mm—his name?

MISS OVINGTON: Dr Charles Alexander Eastman. He
kept glancing up at the sublime arboreal canopy—"my
people worship trees."

DR DU BOIS: I was looking for Dr Eastman to discuss
his paper Native American Tribal Life and he mine, The
Modern Conscience in Relation to the Negro and American
Indian.

MISS OVINGTON: Yes. Both excellent papers. But not one on imperialism. Remember how Annie Besant paced the stage—white hair flying—railing against the British crown— *(She paces and gestures strongly, British accent.)* "Independence for India and Ireland— Independence for India and Ireland—"

DR DU BOIS: Fiercely superb! You've got her! It was a wonderful time! The intention to meet each other, where color is small and unimportant, was totally fulfilled. Where else could dark President Legitime engage in heated discussion with milk-skinned Scandinavians? I want all people of color to feel that freedom of spirit and body!

MISS OVINGTON: The world was hopeful in 1911.

DR DU BOIS: Where did all that hope go?

MISS OVINGTON: *(Slight pause)* May we return to my question of a personal nature?

DR DU BOIS: *(Speaks in French)* Ça depend.

MISS OVINGTON: With whom do you discuss big decisions? Do you have a trusted confidante? You imagined with me, it is my mother. Partly correct. With you, is it Miss Fauset.

DR DU BOIS: Do you find me troubled and in need of a confidante?

MISS OVINGTON: I would not want you to make a decision you would regret because of your— temperament.

DR DU BOIS: *(Irritated)* Thank you, Miss Ovington. I will keep that in mind. At this point it is clear cut. Either the board chooses to regard me as an equal, or I march off into the unknown.

MISS OVINGTON: I don't want to be cross, but is the— *(Slight pause)* Never mind.

DR DU BOIS: Is the what—? There you go again. Hint.
Then withdraw. Is the what—?

MISS OVINGTON: Is the word "compromise" in your
vocabulary?

DR DU BOIS: *(He laughs.)* Speaking of Miss Fauset, her
birthday is approaching. Do you think she might fancy
a scarf like the one you are wearing?

MISS OVINGTON: Certainly—a Parisian silk beauty.

DR DU BOIS: Lord & Taylor?

MISS OVINGTON: A gift.

DR DU BOIS: Will you inquire of the bestower?

MISS OVINGTON: I believe Mister Milholland found it at
Harrod's.

DR DU BOIS: Oh, your Mister Milholland— *(Picks up an
empty pneumatic tube from her desk.)*

MISS OVINGTON: He is not MY Mister Milholland.
He is OUR Mister Milholland. One of the few board
members and philanthropists you and I can always
count on.

DR DU BOIS:—the pneumatic tube man. How fortuitous
to have a capitalist of vision on our side. Mail delivered
in minutes by compressed air. I love technology.

MISS OVINGTON: *(She takes the tube out of his hand and
places it back on her desk)* The pneumatic tube man. I
am sure he would appreciate being called that. *(Slight
pause)* Since you brought up your Miss Fauset, our
Literary Editor, may I speak frankly again?

DR DU BOIS: Dear friend, please. Something more
serious than a heathen or a white hog?

MISS OVINGTON: I cannot believe you did not peruse
each word of the current *Crisis* before it went to press.
Miss Fauset published her poem.

DR DU BOIS: Yes.

MISS OVINGTON: *(She reads the poem to him)*
"Again it is September!
It seems so strange that I who made no vows
Should sit here desolate this golden weather
And wistfully remember
A sign of deepest yearning,
A glowing look and words that knew no bounds,
A swift response, an instant glad surrender
To kisses wild and burning!

Ay me!
Again it is September!
It seems so strange that I who kept those vows
Should sit here lone, and spent, and mutely praying
That I may not remember!"

(DR DU BOIS stares at MISS OVINGTON in silence, arms crossed, shrugs his shoulders, "Well?")

MISS OVINGTON: My heart goes out to her—still young—in love with a married man.

DR DU BOIS: No No—the surrender is to the passion of summer. Seasonal, with an autumnal lament—

MISS OVINGTON: You disequilibrate, Dr Du Bois.

DR DU BOIS: I have never liked that word. You have never heard me use it.

MISS OVINGTON: You should have protected her and not published it. What were you thinking?

DR DU BOIS: Do not tell me this has the board a-chitter chitter chitter.

MISS OVINGTON: No No, not at all. This is me abuzz. Personally. Privately.

DR DU BOIS: Well, I—trust your intentions. *(Getting angry again)* What is YOUR opinion of the institution of marriage? I sense your disapproval that I have betrayed something.

MISS OVINGTON: You tell me. I have never enjoyed the institution.

DR DU BOIS: I think marriage makes a man less available and therefore more appealing.

MISS OVINGTON: Hardly less available. Certainly more available from the man's perspective. I do not know about appealing.

DR DU BOIS: More appealing to certain women because he is not seen as more available.

MISS OVINGTON: Possibly. A woman in love always imagines she will be the one—the new chosen one.

DR DU BOIS: Even when the man declares clearly from the outset, I will never leave my wife.

MISS OVINGTON: Especially then. It is the fate of Zeus, with his trail of ravished earthly maidens and Olympic goddesses, transformed into trees and clouds and endless yearnings.

DR DU BOIS: Mister Milholland is a married man.

MISS OVINGTON: Why do you bring up Mister Milholland?

DR DU BOIS: You are unrestrained in your remarks on Miss Fauset.

MISS OVINGTON: Has there been ugly back room talk?

DR DU BOIS: No. No only my private observations. You and Milholland—exchanged glances—a current of intimacy—suspended—

MISS OVINGTON: What occurred between Mister Milholland and me was rather brief and in the past. He and his daughter serve on our board. His wife has written on women's suffrage for *The Crisis*.

DR DU BOIS: And his wife lives mostly in London.

MISS OVINGTON: Where your wife resides. The wives are in England. War rages. Bombs fall from fantastic flying airships. And you men have your wives in London!

DR DU BOIS: Miss Fauset is a talented, discerning young woman. She would be distressed to know anyone thought her poem had relevance to anyone here.

MISS OVINGTON: "Kisses wild and burning—" That is very specific.

(The phone's brassy ring startles them. MISS OVINGTON *excitedly runs over to the little telephone table.)*

MISS OVINGTON: The telephone. The telephone. *(She sits at the table, lifts the receiver to her ear, speaks slowly and loudly)* Hello? The N A A C P. *(Slight pause)* Yes. Yes. This is Miss Ovington. Hello. N A A C P Chicago, yes, I hear you clearly. Isn't that amazing! *(Slight pause, repeats for* DR DU BOIS*)* Oh, you talked with mother on the home phone. She told you to call here. I am working on a Sunday. Yes. *(She repeats for* DR DU BOIS*.) Birth of a Nation* Chicago premiere last night— thousands protested. Good work!

Arrests. Ah ha! Last week here at Liberty Theatre— can you hear me—as Part Two began when the Klan gallops in on horseback, two men in the audience threw rotten eggs at the screen! *(Slight pause, laughs)* A mess—stopped the moving picture! Oh, we have hundreds outside every night. *(Slight pause)* Bail fund? We are broke as usual. I will see what I can raise. There is a membership salon later at Fannie Villard's. She will contribute, I am certain. *(Slight pause)* Do you want to say hello to Dr Du Bois? He—

*(*DR DU BOIS *sternly signals "no".)*

MISS OVINGTON: —sends his greetings. Yes, this call is running up. Tomorrow, yes. Goodbye. *(Hangs up the receiver)* A marvelous invention! This conversation would take days by post. Now, minutes!

DR DU BOIS: Why did you tell him I was here.

MISS OVINGTON: You are here.

DR DU BOIS: Why does he have to know we are together in the office on a Sunday morning?

MISS OVINGTON: Oh, he would not think that way.

DR DU BOIS: He is very conservative.

MISS OVINGTON: He mobilized a huge demonstration.

DR DU BOIS: *(Sarcastic)* Oh, of course.

MISS OVINGTON: I will never be able to watch Lillian Gish again. She had me weeping in *The Angel of Contention.* How could she agree to be the star attraction in *Birth*—

DR DU BOIS: A K K K recruitment film!

MISS OVINGTON: An N A A C P recruitment film!

DR DU BOIS: Seventy lynchings this year!

MISS OVINGTON: And last year! And the year before that!

(MISS OVINGTON *jumps when an egg, thrown through the open window, lands on the floor just missing her.)*

MISS OVINGTON: Ohhh! An egg! What a mess!

DR DU BOIS: *(She leans out of the window.)* Stay back. He may throw a paving stone.

MISS OVINGTON: Look! There he is! *(Calls down)* You! Come up here! Say what you have to say in words not eggs! We have literature and enlightenment.

DR DU BOIS: It is not the lynch flag. It is us. Picture their worst fear—social equality. A black man and a white woman together in a window frame. Let us pose. Arrangement in Black and White. That is what Whistler would call us.

MISS OVINGTON: *(Steps away from the window)* Watch out! *(She catches an egg that breaks in her hand.)* Ahhh.

DR DU BOIS: Good catch!

(An egg whizzes by DR DU BOIS's head.)

MISS OVINGTON: *(She points down to the street, and calls down.)* Stop that! Stop wasting eggs *(To him, holds up her "egg hand".)* I would like to rub this egg in his face.

DR DU BOIS: *(Leans out of the window, looks down)* He is going. Back to church. Back to pray to his God. *(Calls down)* Good white Christian gentleman. You have upheld the glorious traditions of Anglo-Saxon manhood!

MISS OVINGTON: Not your linen handkerchief. There are tea towels in my bottom drawer.

(Before MISS OVINGTON stoops down to clean up the eggs on the floor, DR DU BOIS and MISS OVINGTON pause, look at each other.)

MISS OVINGTON: *Oeufs.*

DR DU BOIS: *Oeufs—brouilles.*

MISS OVINGTON: *Oeufs—au plat. (She rises.)* I will take these to the washroom. At least they are fresh, not rotten. *(Slight pause)* A thousand daily indignities. You must be so tired of it.

R DU BOIS: Not a tragedy, Miss Ovington. A sting. A scratch.

MISS OVINGTON: It is frightening how race prejudice steadily increases.

DR DU BOIS: While internally my people are taking great steps forward.

Clare Coss   31

Two movements brimming with future danger.

MISS OVINGTON: Are you afraid walking on the street?

DR DU BOIS: I am a moving target. But I reject fear.
Only during the Atlanta race riots was I afraid for the
life of my son, should the mob storm onto campus.
Nina and I taught Burghardt to hide in back of the
closet as a game. He remained very still until we called,
"All clear!" We thought it might save his life one day.

MISS OVINGTON: Is it as hard to be of a despised race as
of a race that does despicable deeds.

DR DU BOIS: Miss Ovington, my deepest fear is that
I may miss an opportunity to speak out. To my great
relief, I say what I think, not what I think I ought to
think, but what I actually think. (Slight pause) Look
at our map. Every free American citizen enjoys the
inalienable right to be lynched without tiresome
investigation and penalties.

MISS OVINGTON: How many mothers feel, when my
son goes out, I want him to come home—safe.

DR DU BOIS: Or when their daughters go out. (Looks
back at the map) Is there a pin in Marietta, Georgia for
Leo Frank?

MISS OVINGTON: Of course.

(DR DU BOIS finds it.)

DR DU BOIS: Most likely innocent of rape and murder
of the factory girl. Fair game because he was a Jew.

MISS OVINGTON: Mary Phagan was thirteen years old.

DR DU BOIS: The same age as my daughter.

MISS OVINGTON: Oh, the mail! I forgot! You have an
overseas letter from Yolande and one from Mrs Du
Bois, I believe. (Indicating the corner of her desk) Over
there—I was going to place them on your blotter. How
is she doing in her English school?

(The Westminster bell chimes play the three quarter melody.)

DR DU BOIS: *(Picking up a silver letter opener from her desk.)* May I? By the by, I admired your poem, *Mary Phagan Speaks*. Where did I read it?

MISS OVINGTON: *The New Republic.*

DR DU BOIS: Ah, yes. Did you submit it to Miss Fauset?

MISS OVINGTON: No. You publish me so often—. It must be hard on you and your wife far away from each other for Yolande's school years.

DR DU BOIS: Bedales *(Pronounced: BEE dulls)* was my wife's idea as well as mine. It is innovative and progressive: head, hand, heart. Good for her.

MISS OVINGTON: Are there other students of color— from the empire?

DR DU BOIS: No, alas. Not currently. *(Reads out loud)* "Dear Papa, Today is mama's birthday. She came down for the weekend from London. A Zeppelin passed over Bedales last night. It dropped bombs on Guildford, a town not very far away. We have dark curtains on the windows. I have just finished making a dress for poor children and am knitting a scarf for soldiers." *(Scans down quickly)* Not a word about her lessons.

MISS OVINGTON: Is she afraid living in a war zone?

DR DU BOIS: Miss Ovington, she is getting along just fine.

MISS OVINGTON: Bombs dropping nearby. That doesn't sound fine. Does she talk about her—

DR DU BOIS: *(Interrupting)* She complains only of the hardships war brings, such as food rations, curfews. Daughter is enjoying an excellent education and Wife is nearby making it possible.

MISS OVINGTON: I did not mean to imply—

DR DU BOIS: *(He slips Yolande's letter and his wife's unopened letter in his breast pocket.)* Having lost one child, I would certainly not place another child in danger.

MISS OVINGTON: Of course not. I am sorry, Dr Du Bois. It is heartening to receive news, even a month old.

DR DU BOIS: If need be, the telegraph takes minutes. They are safe in England, Miss Ovington.

MISS OVINGTON: *(Explodes)* No one is safe any more. I awake happy to see the sun streaming through my window. A second later, I think of youth killing youth, maiming, blinding, crippling, gassing, burning homes, lush forests cut down, barbed wire everywhere—war, Dr Du Bois. You and I are Pacifists. War is murder. You called it that in your Credo.

DR DU BOIS: *(An angry exchange ensues)* War *is* murder. War is worse than hell. And this new desperate rampage to carve up Africa gives the Europeans a new name: barbarians. *(Stops himself, pulls back)* But when the U S joins up, our boys are going to cross the color line and serve along with other American citizens.

MISS OVINGTON: Exercising their right to be slaughtered, like other American citizens.

DR DU BOIS: You said that before.

MISS OVINGTON: You said that before, too.

DR DU BOIS: Go. Go. I am sorry to have detained you with your hands full of broken shells and dripping yokes.

*(*MISS OVINGTON *exits swiftly with the wet egg cloths. To himself:)*

DR DU BOIS: Bombs away, Miss Ovington! Woman! *(Slight pause)* They are safe in England.

(The sudden piercing ring of the telephone surprises DR
DU BOIS. *He reaches his hand out in the direction of* MISS
OVINGTON *to call her back. Answers the phone reluctantly.)*
DR DU BOIS: N A A C P. *(Slight pause, relieved to hear it is*
MISS OVINGTON's *mother on the line)* Ah, Mrs Ovington.
Mrs. Ann Louisa Ovington. How lovely to hear your
voice. She is—here—yes, but—she is—indisposed—
down the hall. How are you, dear lady? Yes, yes,
Chicago called. *(Slight pause)* Your daughter will raise
bail money for them, never fear. We improvise here.
(Slight pause) Miss Ovington knows everyone. She has
infinite contacts. *(Slight pause)* Her prerogative to take
on new—I cannot stop her.
Slow her down? *(He laughs.)* It WAS a difficult board
meeting. *(Slight pause)* Dear Lady, I am not trying to
kill your daughter. She and I are absolute allies when it
comes to my quarrel for autonomy. This call is running
up. Perhaps we best say farewell. A pleasure always.
Goodbye. Goodbye. *(Slight pause)* Pardon? My newest?
The Negro. That is the title. Simply, *The Negro. (Slight
pause, pleased)* The first sentence? "Africa is at once the
most romantic and the most tragic of continents." You
shall have a copy. Good day, my dear lady. Good day.
*(He hangs up, enters his office, rolls his chair in front of the
Dictophone puts the wax cylinder in place. Sits back for a
moment. Quickly reads the letter from his daughter. Clicks
on the Dictaphone.)* Miss Randolph, good morning,
Miss Randolph. I trust you spent a pleasant weekend.
I return to the office Tuesday morning. *(Slight pause,
re-reads a few lines from Yolanda's letter)* First letter. To
Yolanda. *(Begins to dictate)*
Dearest Daughter,
You must know that brown is as pretty as white or
prettier and crinkly hair is as pretty as straight, even
though it is harder to comb.
I am enclosing the latest *Crisis* because it is about

our people—your people and mine, whom we must
love and of whom we must be proud. Show it to the
girls and never be ashamed of your folk. Above all
remember: your father loves you and believes in you
and expects you to be a wonderful woman. Study hard.
Concentrate. Do your lessons.
Lovingly yours,
Papa.
(He clicks it off, then clicks it on)
Miss Randolph, please address this to Miss Mary
White Ovington.
Dear Miss Ovington,
I write to you because you are one of the few persons
whom I call Friend.
(He clicks off the microphone. Plays back his words.)
"I write to you because you are one of the few persons
whom I call Friend."
(He clicks it off. He clicks it on.)

Why is sharing power with a Negro so totally out of
the question? *(He plays it back.)*

DICTAPHONE: Why is sharing power with a Negro so
totally out of the question?

(DR DU BOIS plays it back.)

I write to you because you are one of the few persons
whom I call Friend.

(Puts the Dictaphone down, muses)

DR DU BOIS: I wonder, Miss Ovington, is the scent you
are wearing—lavender? From Provence?

MISS OVINGTON: *(She returns, sees his door is closed,
goes to her desk, rolls a piece of paper into her typewriter.
She speaks as she types. After her typing is established, she
continues to speak without typing.)*
Dear Chairman Spingarn,
I am still smarting from your accusations of idolatry.

You unkindly called me silly.
Said that I coddle Dr Du Bois. Your sudden demand
for supreme power over the Association, your proposal
for the odious Committee of Three, is silly. You have to
give on your side, and Dr Du Bois, I believe, will find
his way to give on his side.
*(She pulls the page out and rolls in a blank paper, speaking
out loud as she types.)*
Dear Dr Du Bois, Dear Friend,
(She stops typing, sits back in her chair.) At the window
when you held me by the waist—an amorous wave
engulfed me. *(Looks at his door, muses)* Is your beard
soft? Not wiry and scratchy like my brother's. It
looks soft. *(Slight pause)* Your Credo: "I believe in the
freedom to choose friends, enjoy the sunshine and
ride on the railroads, uncursed by color. *(Slight pause)*
My Credo: We can criticize a black man for legitimate
shortcomings and champion his right to be treated as
fully human.

*(The lighting shifts to focus on each at their desks. In
an interwoven duet, DR DU BOIS and MISS OVINGTON
individually reflect on the childhood moment of coming to
race consciousness.)*

DR DU BOIS: I remember well when the shadow swept
across me. I was a little thing, away up in the hills of
New England, where the dark Housatonic River winds
to the sea.

MISS OVINGTON: One day my mother took me to a new
dressmaker down by the East River. The woman's face
was dark and lovely, her accent lilting and lyrical. On
the way home I asked mother, is she colored?

DR DU BOIS: In a wee wooden schoolhouse, something
put it into the boys' and girls' heads to buy gorgeous
visiting cards—ten cents a package—and exchange.

MISS OVINGTON: My mother snapped, No, May, of course not, she is West Indian. I was shocked at mother's fierce rebuke.

DR DU BOIS: The exchange was merry, till one girl, a tall newcomer, refused my card peremptorily, with a glance. It dawned on me with a suddenness that I was different from the others; alike in heart and life, and longing, but shut out from their world by a vast veil.

MISS OVINGTON: I was bewildered. What was my mother teaching me? The dressmaker was the first colored person I had ever been with.

DR DU BOIS: One ever feels this duality—an American, a Negro; two souls, two thoughts, two unreconciled longings—

MISS OVINGTON: We had the Emancipation Proclamation on the dining room wall. We celebrated Harriet Tubman and Sojourner Truth at home. But actually being with a colored woman was a problem.

DR DU BOIS: —two warring ideals in one dark body— whose dogged strength alone keeps it from being torn asunder.

MISS OVINGTON: Even talking about being with a colored woman was forbidden.

DR DU BOIS:	MISS OVINGTON:
We meet in the between	—the between territory,
territory, Miss Ovington.	Dr Du Bois.

(The lights shift back to full. MISS OVINGTON *looks in the direction of* DR DU BOIS's *office, pulls out two silver tablespoons from her desk drawer and begins to "play the spoons" haltingly. Tries to get them going. He looks up from the papers on his desk and listens. He leaves his office and approaches her with a delighted "May I?" gesture.)*

MISS OVINGTON: Are you about to reveal that you are proficient at spoons?

DR DU BOIS: With your permission.

(MISS OVINGTON *hands them to* DR DU BOIS. *He pulls a chair over, sits next to her.*)

DR DU BOIS: Spoons! It will come back! (*He plays them enthusiastically for a moment.*) When I was a student at Fisk, I taught for two summers in the deep backwoods plantation area of Eastern Tennessee. I walked for days in search of children in need of a teacher. One morning on the road I encountered Young Josie, "You be the first colored teacher ever dropped down in our little world." Her mother took me in and I reopened their abandoned schoolroom.

MISS OVINGTON: Were they not lucky!

DR DU BOIS: No electricity. Long dark evenings until dawn.

MISS OVINGTON: To learn the spoons and sing and enjoy the music of the spheres. One of my great fascinations is the night sky.

DR DU BOIS: Josie's mother, shall we say, "initiated" the shy young man.

MISS OVINGTON: I can picture you "shy"—as a young man.

DR DU BOIS: (*Quickly*) I taught my young charges Cicero's *Pro Archia Poeta* to help their own fight for full citizenship.

MISS OVINGTON: Cicero! In grade school I carried around Herbert Spencer's First Principles to defy my teacher who rejected Darwin's theory of evolution. "The world was created in six days," she insisted.

(DR DU BOIS *continues playing.* MISS OVINGTON *claps in time with his 4/4 rhythm.*)

MISS OVINGTON: I was trying to show Dihdwo Twe how to play and could not get them going.

DR DU BOIS: Practice. Practice.

MISS OVINGTON: *(She starts singing "Balling the Jack"
in time to his beat, rises from her chair, performs a lithe,
flirtatious dance to match the words.)*
Now first you put your two knees
Close up tight
Then you sway to the left
Then you sway to the right.
Step around the floor kind of nice and light
Then you twist around and twist around
With all of your might.
Stretch your lovin' arms straight out in space
Then you do the eagle rock with style and grace.
Swing your foot way round and bring it back
Now that's what I call ballin' the jack!

(On the last line MISS OVINGTON *turns and lands back in
her chair, next to* DR DU BOIS. *They laugh, enjoying the
moment.)*

DR DU BOIS: Graceful and light of step—very ladylike
ragtime.

MISS OVINGTON: Ladylike ?

DR DU BOIS: Well, you are a lady. How about a waltz
one evening?

MISS OVINGTON: I love to waltz.

DR DU BOIS: One, two, three.

MISS OVINGTON: One, two, three. *(Slight pause)* Did you
ever hear *Balling the Jack* before?

DR DU BOIS: I heard Buddy Bradley perform it for the
first time at Harlem's Darktown Follies. "Balling the
Jack"—railroad slang for movin' fast down the tracks.

MISS OVINGTON: I thought I had you on this one.

DR DU BOIS: Turned out I had you. You want to learn
the spoons.

MISS OVINGTON: I can pick it up if you just get me started.

DR DU BOIS: *(He demonstrates how to hold the spoons back to back , separated by the index finger. He holds his other hand a few inches above his thigh and starts playing, hitting the spoons from his raised hand down to his thigh.)* Here, hold them like this. Down on your thigh. Up on your palm. Down on your thigh. Up on your palm. Get that click. The click. Click. *(Stops, hands the spoons to her)* Here, you try now.

(DR DU BOIS hands MISS OVINGTON the spoons and starts to adjust her hold on them. Their four hands clasp together in an embrace that releases an overpowering desire between them. Their faces very close, they do not move. He whispers.)

DR DU BOIS: Lavender.

MISS OVINGTON: *(Gently caresses his beard, whispers)* Silk.

(DR DU BOIS and MISS OVINGTON whisper each other's nicknames.)

DR DU BOIS: May.

MISS OVINGTON: Will.

(DR DU BOIS and MISS OVINGTON stay close, feel each other's breath. Neither one moves in for the kiss. They are spellbound.)

DR DU BOIS: *(Whispers)* I'm going to step out for a cigarette.

MISS OVINGTON: *(Not moving)* I appreciate you have not lit up in front of me.

DR DU BOIS: *(Still close)* Oh, but I have. *(He slowly pulls away and stands up)* Excuse me. *(He exits.)*

(MISS OVINGTON watches DR DU BOIS go, smiles to herself. The lights dim. She imagines a fully orchestrated Strauss waltz slowly increase in volume. He re-enters in this dream sequence, sweeps her into his arms for a few turns of a

stylish waltz. As the music fades, he disappears, closing the door behind him. She enjoys her reverie for a moment.)

(The lights come up.)

*(*Dr Du Bois *comes bounding in with two small cone-shaped paper cups of crushed flavored ices.)*

Dr Du Bois: *(Hands her a cup)* Strawberry snowballs—to cool us off.

Miss Ovington: Thank you. My favorite flavor. Lemon is quite thirst quenching, too.

*(*Dr Du Bois *and* Miss Ovington *stand, take a few bites, looking at each other.)*

Miss Ovington: That was—a close call.

Dr Du Bois: *(He laughs lightly.)* For now.

Miss Ovington: *(Smiles)* Forever.

*(*Dr Du Bois *and* Miss Ovington *toast with their snowballs.)*

Dr Du Bois: What stopped you?

Miss Ovington: Why did you not go ahead?

Dr Du Bois: Why did not you?

Miss Ovington: You are the man.

Dr Du Bois: Oh, Miss Ovington, women's rights!

*(*Miss Ovington *laughs.)*

Dr Du Bois: For me—I—I gave this thought when I was down on the street. Of course, I believe in social equality and advocate to repeal the laws against intermarriage. The mystery of chemistry and stirrings lead us every which way. A black man may marry any sane, grown person who wants to marry him. But where is our loyalty at this moment as we confront barriers? A black man with a white woman is easily accused of being ashamed of his race, of wanting social recognition.

MISS OVINGTON: Are you saying you were stopped by race pride?

DR DU BOIS: Exactly. Race pride. It is race pride that fights for freedom.

MISS OVINGTON: An entire history separates you and me—a chasm of harrowing depths filled with slavery—lynchings—brutality—deprivation—the worst in human nature.

DR DU BOIS: You are upset.

MISS OVINGTON: I cannot suppress the woman in me.

DR DU BOIS: I am sorry. It is not personal.

MISS OVINGTON: It is personal, because I care about you, our failure to—kiss. There I used the word.

DR DU BOIS: Why did you stop?

MISS OVINGTON: My hesitation was based on practicality. How could we possibly work together in this office? How could I see you walk out the door with Miss Fauset on your arm and not feel like shouting out, "you're too young for him. Leave him to me." For me, let's call it: Work Pride. We have to keep this organization strong, and a personal weakness on my part is not going to bring it down.

DR DU BOIS: *(Quietly)* May—admirable.

(MISS OVINGTON *is struck with an idea that pleases her.)*

DR DU BOIS: What are you thinking?

MISS OVINGTON: During my courtship days, I dragged a young suitor to hear Frederick Douglass speak at Cooper Union. He didn't want to go. I told him, "Douglas is brilliant, majestic, looks like Aesop—"

DR DU BOIS: You thought I looked like "Shakespeare in bronze' when we first met.

MISS OVINGTON: I still do. My date was shocked when I told him, "Mr. Douglass is married to a white woman. He claims his first wife, who died, was a woman the color of his mother. His second wife is the color of his father." This was 1885. I didn't know then that Douglass had also dallied with two white suffragists— concurrently. I do not want to be a footnote as a great man's dalliance. *Vive la Resistance!*

DR DU BOIS: *(Smiles)* Good. Very good—Miss Ovington. My wife, fortunately for me, is the color of my mother and my father. *(Slight pause)* Why did you never marry? *(Slight pause)* What about John Milholland? If I may ask.

MISS OVINGTON: I know Mister Milholland dabbles with other women. But with me, he wanted to leave his wife, and that was not possible. He suffered so—I said, let's just stop. Your wife and daughter are part of our team here—. We will be friends and allies as before— nothing more.

DR DU BOIS: That must have been hard for both of you.

MISS OVINGTON: He was relieved. And you know I am called a saint. Yes. It was hard. I have never talked about this with anyone, ever. Please—

DR DU BOIS: *(Touches his heart)* Safely locked away.

MISS OVINGTON: May I ask, what happened between you and Mrs Du Bois? You are seldom together geographically.

DR DU BOIS: When our son, Burghardt, died of diphtheria in Atlanta, two and a half years old, our marriage died, too, in a sense. She blamed me for moving us South, to the land of Jim Crow and terror. His fever raged out of control. White doctors turned us away. We could not find a physician of our own race. Nina has never forgiven me. Torn asunder by grief and blame.

MISS OVINGTON: What has it done to your heart? The ravages of race in America—

DR DU BOIS: My heart? My heart keeps a steady call for the greater voice—to seek what is right amidst the gloom and horror of life.

MISS OVINGTON: Whites, we—need a revolution to ignite our humanity—our compassion—to lead us beyond brutality, indifference, silence—the turning away from a feverish child.

DR DU BOIS: We live in a world where so-called "normal" white people have no regard for the life, the souls, social conditions, degradation, sanctity of African blood. Where are the white people who care, Miss Ovington?

MISS OVINGTON: The progressives on our board are open.

DR DU BOIS: Yes, but except for them, and a handful scattered across the country, where is the white financial support we anticipated at our inception? No. Nickels, dimes, and quarters flow in from membership dues and contributions from colored folk in the branches from New York to California. Where is the white rank and file, as it were. Where are they? In church on Sunday morning, the most segregated hour of the week? In labor unions that refuse to admit the Negro? In the Socialist party that spurns the Negro? In women's suffrage, demanding the vote for white women only?

MISS OVINGTON: Part of our work is to make inroads into liberal white bastions.

DR DU BOIS: Liberal. Except when it comes to the Negro. You have a romance about white people and their habits of responsibility. Look what I have had to put up with right here in our organization. Oswald Garrison Villard for one. Our famous railroad millionaire greeted me here on my first day up from Atlanta. *(He imitates an upper class accent.)* "I do not know who's going to pay your salary. I have no money."

MISS OVINGTON: That was five years ago. We have—

DR DU BOIS: *(Interrupts)* Don't forget Villard's insulting, inaccurate derisive review of my John Brown biography. And you, too, Miss Ovington, were shocked and disgusted by his insistence that we list the names of black criminals next to the names of lynched men in my Burden column. Oh, Mister Villard, have you a list of white men lynched?

MISS OVINGTON: The entire board rejected that immediately and unanimously. Villard is a worthy ally. Give him credit where due—four face to face meetings with Wilson to stop his re-segregation of Washington and—

DR DU BOIS: *(Interrupts)* His wife, Julia Breckenridge Sanford, prized Georgia debutante, still refuses to allow a Negro or a Jew in their home. He and I are close intellectually. I had thought—we would be friends. How does a patrician of high principle anchor himself to a bigot? *(Highly agitated)* My God, Villard's mother, Mrs Fannie Villard, welcomes me to her table. Have you ever dined at the Oswald Garrison Villards?

MISS OVINGTON: You know he does not socialize with any of us here.

DR DU BOIS: Have you crossed his threshold?

MISS OVINGTON: His Jim Crow threshold? Never! Please Dr Du Bois. Settle down. We spurn the likes of southern debutants who revel in extreme wealth, luxury and hate.

DR DU BOIS: When I address a white audience, large or small, on, say, the disenfranchisement of my people, I brace my soul for the aftermath. A cold green-eyed lady approaches, "Do you know where I can get a good colored cook?" Why do the minds of so many decent and up-seeing folk view the entire Negro problem as a matter of their getting a cook or a maid? Any white man of decency would rather cut his daughter's throat than let her grow up to a destiny of menial work and enforced sexual relations. *(Slight pause)* White people assume we have no common humanity.

MISS OVINGTON: That breaks down when we get to know each other. Human contact, human sympathy, human friendship are the great solvents of human problems!

(DR DU BOIS steps into his office, MISS OVINGTON follows.)

DR DU BOIS: Why do I continue to work here without the full support of the board behind me?
Excuse me, Miss Ovington. I have a train to catch.

MISS OVINGTON: We must not give up hope.

DR DU BOIS: Now, Miss Randolph—

MISS OVINGTON: Dr Du Bois, do not lose faith in our work here.

DR DU BOIS: *(Loses his temper, speaks fiercely in French)* Silence! *(Pronounced see-LONCE!)* Taisez-vous! *(Pronounced tez a—VOO)* Silence! Not another word from you!

MISS OVINGTON: Do not order me to hush-up in any language!

DR DU BOIS: *(He sits at the Dictaphone, struggles to control his agitation.)* Tais-toi! *(Pronounced tay-TWAH)* Remove yourself from my presence ! Let me dictate! *(Clicks on the microphone)* Now, Miss Randolph.

MISS OVINGTON: Miss Randolph, Dr Du Bois has lost his temper!

DR DU BOIS: *(He clicks off the Dictaphone)* Now my letter to Yolanda is lost, thanks to you. *(He grabs the cylinder and starts to shave it.)*

MISS OVINGTON: Do not shave it all away. Give Miss Randolph a little Monday morning entertainment.

DR DU BOIS: You have forced me to lose my temper!

MISS OVINGTON: It was not my intention to provoke you—

DR DU BOIS: *(Fiercely) Silence!!!! (French pronunciation: see—LONCE. He picks up the Dictaphone tube, regains his composure, and begins to record.)* Miss Randolph, on the desk you will find my revised demands to the board. Please incorporate them into my standard resignation letter. One: I refuse to have my time and expenses monitored. Two: I am the exclusive editor of *The Crisis*. Three: I report to the full board, not a Committee of Three. Please post to each member—

(MISS OVINGTON starts waving furiously. DR DU BOIS clicks off the Dictaphone.)

MISS OVINGTON: *(Declaims seriously)* Let not the die be cast.

DR DU BOIS: Caesar crossing the Rubicon. I like it.

MISS OVINGTON: *(Whispers)* Do not mock me.

DR DU BOIS: Never. Never. *(He clicks it back on, speaks into the microphone.)* Miss Randolph—add the following:

(DR DU BOIS *indicates for* MISS OVINGTON *to come close to him. Looks directly at her while he speaks.*)

DR DU BOIS: I demand a full man's chance to complete a work without chains and petty hampering. In the white world, the man of ability and integrity has the right to make mistakes if the final result justifies his effort. The colored man gets no such chance. Even when his ability is patent it is "inexpedient" to trust him.

To the board, Miss Randolph, send to the board. *(He clicks it off, stands up and puts the cover on the Dictaphone.)* What do you think? You asked if I have a confidante? What do you think?

MISS OVINGTON: It is important for you to say what you have to say. You must continually suffer more than any of us who see through white eyes can imagine.

DR DU BOIS: I, who avoid the company of white people except when absolutely necessary, find myself here at this moment with you, Miss Ovington, giving me hope.

MISS OVINGTON: Please give me hope. *(Slight pause)* Can we save what we are struggling to build.

DR DU BOIS: That is not up to me.

MISS OVINGTON: *(Tries to hold back her fury)* Friction. Friction. Friction. Our files brim over with letters. You to me. Me to you. Villard to me, you to Villard, Spingarn to me, me to Spingarn. I'm going to resign. No, I'm going to resign. No, I'm going to resign. How do we accomplish our crucial work in this atmosphere.

DR DU BOIS: We have excellent staff on all fronts. You keep everything going.

MISS OVINGTON: Chairman Spingarn—

DR DU BOIS: *(Interrupts)* Chairman Spingarn is a dynamic leader whom I respect. Only you can bring him around to his senses regarding me.

MISS OVINGTON: So there is no meeting Spingarn half way.

DR DU BOIS: Half way means becoming a white man's organization that works for the interests of colored people in which no colored person has any real power.

(Hears the clock chime)

DR DU BOIS: My train—

MISS OVINGTON: To quote Ecclesiastes: Better than the dead or living "is he which hath not been." A finer way to say, I wish I had never been born.

DR DU BOIS: Miss Ovington, don't YOU give up. We progress. On Tuesday we celebrate our first Supreme Court triumph favoring black voters in Oklahoma.

MISS OVINGTON: I am tired of the friction, all the pulls in every direction.

DR DU BOIS: Remember how you and I fought against the conservatives who wanted Booker Washington on board. Now he is ill and dying and there is talk of unity. The N A A C P is a bridge—vital to—

MISS OVINGTON: *(Interrupts)* Vital—as long as we learn to go along with your strong will.

DR DU BOIS: I cannot be denied the right to exercise judgment.

(MISS OVINGTON turns away.)

DR DU BOIS: Look at me. Please. You are the visionary who had the idea for this organization! You are the one holding us together with both hands and both feet and your entire heart.

MISS OVINGTON: I can let go.

DR DU BOIS: You cannot let go.

MISS OVINGTON: When you invited me, the only white person, to join the John Brown pilgrimage to walk at dawn, barefoot, in silence, candles cupped against the breeze, to the top of the hill at Harper's Ferry—infused with the belief in the equality of all human beings on this earth—when— (*She struggles to keep her composure, waves him away.*) I refuse to let you make me miserable.

DR DU BOIS: I do not want you to be miserable.

MISS OVINGTON: (*Angry*) I am miserable.

DR DU BOIS: I am sorry.

MISS OVINGTON: (*More angry*) You are never sorry.

DR DU BOIS: What can I do?

MISS OVINGTON: (*Anger builds*) What can we do? I do not feature living at home with mother, serving on boards, a maiden lady do-gooder, when I can have an impact on the future of our nation right here.

DR DU BOIS: You will have a roof over your head. Food and wine at your table.

MISS OVINGTON: (*Still angry*) What will you look forward to each morning when you awaken, without your base. Without *The Crisis*.

DR DU BOIS: I will drown myself—in the utter joy of life.

MISS OVINGTON: Indeed. (*She laughs.*) How dare you make me laugh at this moment. I hate you.

DR DU BOIS: You do?

MISS OVINGTON: I do. I really do. (*Slight pause*) Dr Du Bois, I will serve on the misguided Committee of Three.

DR DU BOIS: You will serve thus?

MISS OVINGTON: Yes, I will serve "thus."

DR DU BOIS: *(Deeply touched)* My dear Miss Ovington— *(Calculated pause)* Let us agree. *(He springs it on her.)* I report only to YOU on the Committee of Three.

(MISS OVINGTON *hesitates a moment, extends her hand and she and* DR DU BOIS *shake, savoring their hard-won negotiation.)*

DR DU BOIS: My train!

MISS OVINGTON: What about your instructions to Miss Randolph?

DR DU BOIS: Ah! Resignation Letter Number Four will continue to reside in my breast pocket.

(DR DU BOIS *strides into his office, removes the wax cylinder.* MISS OVINGTON *is at the window. He heads for the door.)*

MISS OVINGTON: Will?

DR DU BOIS: *(He goes to her.)* What? May. What? Are you sorry you made me lose my temper?

MISS OVINGTON: I was going to say I don't hate you any more, but now I am not so sure.

DR DU BOIS: What were you going to say?

MISS OVINGTON: I sincerely believe that we humans are still evolving. We are not even half finished.

One day it might be better for woman and man on this earth.

DR DU BOIS: The mighty human rainbow of the world agrees. Still, Miss Ovington, the problem of the twentieth century is the problem of the color line.

MISS OVINGTON: Yes. *(Slight pause)* Greet the mountains for me.

DR DU BOIS: *(Reaches for her hat)* Your hat.

MISS OVINGTON: *(She walks back to her desk.)* No, no. I am leaving later. Fannie Villard's new member salon is at two. Dihdwo Twe is joining me there.

DR DU BOIS: *(He sets down his briefcase, walks toward her, extends his hand to her, palm up.)* Dihdwo Twe. Peace is planted between us.

MISS OVINGTON: *(She clasps his hand with both her hands. They look at each other steadily. They take a few breaths, then she speaks.)* Dihdwo Twe.

(After a moment, DR DU BOIS turns, puts on his hat, picks up his briefcase and exits. MISS OVINGTON walks back to her typewriter. She rolls in a fresh piece of paper, and speaks out loud as she begins to type.)

MISS OVINGTON: Dear Chairman Spingarn,
You like to tell Dr Du Bois that he must cease to be obstinate. *(Stops typing, looks up, speaks)* You must learn how to use his obstinacy, for he and *The Crisis* are indispensable to us here. Dr Du Bois is the master builder whose work will speak to us as long as there is an oppressed race on earth. *(Slight pause)* But to be the only Negro holding executive office puts unfair pressure on him. We must shift to black leadership on every level, from the branches to the position of chair. *(She pointedly enjoys her emphasis on the word "chair".)*

(Black out)

END OF PLAY

Do ba-na co-ba, ge-ne me, ge-ne me!

Do ba-na co-ba, ge-ne me, ge-ne me!

Ben d' nu-li, nu-li, nu-li, nu-li, ben d' le.